"One man's trash is
a grouch's treasure."
—*Socrates*

THE PURSUIT OF GROUCHINESS

OSCAR THE GROUCH'S GUIDE TO LIFE

BY <u>ME</u>, OSCAR, who else?!

SESAME STREET

[Imprint]
MAKE YOUR MARK

NEW YORK

[Imprint]
MAKE YOUR MARK

A part of Macmillan Publishing Group, LLC
175 Fifth Avenue, New York, NY 10010

THE PURSUIT OF GROUCHINESS: OSCAR THE GROUCH'S GUIDE TO LIFE.
Copyright © 2019 by Sesame Workshop. Sesame Street® and associated characters,
trademarks and design elements are owned and licensed by Sesame Workshop.
All rights reserved. Printed in China by RR Donnelley Asia Printing Solutions Ltd.,
Dongguan City, Guangdong Province.

Library of Congress Cataloging-in-Publication Data is available.

ISBN 978-1-250-30454-4 (hardcover)

Our books may be purchased in bulk for promotional, educational, or business use.
Please contact your local bookseller or the Macmillan Corporate and Premium
Sales Department at (800) 221-7945 ext. 5442 or
by email at MacmillanSpecialMarkets@macmillan.com.

Special thanks to Julie Kraut

Book design by Ellen Duda
Imprint logo designed by Amanda Spielman

1 3 5 7 9 10 8 6 4 2

Steal not this book, my grumpy pal,
Or else be warned your own locale
Will be overrun with stinky trash.
Do not steal! Grouches pay in cash!

TO ME,

for putting up with all of you.
Now that takes dedication.

PART

A FEW of MY LEAST FAVORITE THINGS

YOU'RE LUCKY TO BE READING THIS, YOU KNOW.

It's not every day I spend valuable grouchy time writing trashy stuff like this.

SOME MOMENTS ARE PRICELESS.

Not this one.

BE THE GROUCH you WISH to see in the WORLD.

You think you're in a bad mood? MY NAME IS OSCAR THE GROUCH, AND I LIVE IN A TRASH CAN.

The **TERM** is "GROUCH," BUT **I** will ACCEPT "GRUMP."

People always ask me about Sesame Street
like it's this great place or something.
I've lived on worse streets.

I miss those days.

MONDAY IS MY FAVORITE.

It's when everyone's the grouchiest.

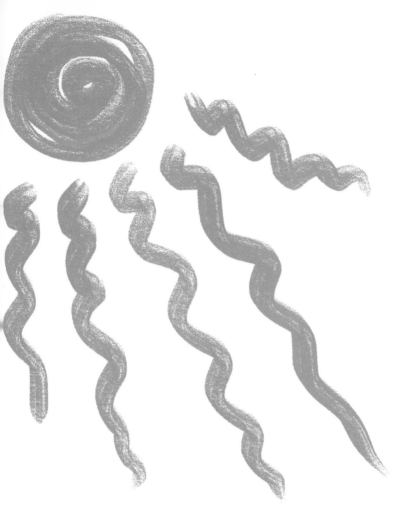

People ask if I'm
allergic to sunshine.
I'm just sunshine intolerant.

I like rainbows better in
BLACK AND WHITE.

This year, it was great—we went right from

AWFUL SNOWSTORMS . . .

I always get nervous when
I'm finishing a jigsaw puzzle.

WHAT IF THERE ISN'T
A PIECE MISSING?

Thanks for asking,
but I'm getting enough sleep.

THIS IS JUST WHO I AM.

I like diamonds better
when they are still

White is my favorite color.

It really shows the

STAINS.

We're grouches.
We can only be happy when it rains.

My favorite gift is one that gives you

A PAPER CUT

when you're unwrapping it.

Frowning makes me happy.

CAN'T YOU TELL?

Psst.
All your lost socks?
I've got them. You're welcome.

TRASH.

Great for regifting.

WANT TO KNOW MY IDEA OF FUN?

Hanging out at the airport.
It always does the trick,
especially around the holidays.

Even I can't be grouchy all the time.
Sometimes I'm downright miserable.

Some people try to live every day like
it's their best day ever.
I live every day like it's my worst ever.

So . . . I guess I live my best day?

And that makes it my worst?

Which . . .

AH, WHATEVER!

All I know is, it works like a charm.

i GROUCH, THEREFORE you SCRAM.

PART 2

GROUCH LIFE

All you really need in life is

A CAN,
A PET WORM,
A PILE OF TRASH,
AND PEOPLE TO ANNOY.

Oh yeah, and a pickle 'n' fish ice-cream float.

As long as I can look back and say,

"THERE'S NO WAY I COULD HAVE BEEN GROUCHIER,"

it was a good day.

If you're looking for morning cheer,
YOU'RE AT THE WRONG CAN.

Just saw a beautiful sunrise outside
and it inspired me . . .

TO GET UP AND CLOSE THE CURTAINS.

I try to wake up on the
wrong side of the bed
EVERY MORNING.

(It helps that I have a bed
with two wrong sides.
I paid extra for it.)

My goal is to have morning breath

ALL DAY LONG.

They tell me to be more cheerful.

NOT A CHANCE.

How would anybody recognize me?

If I wake up feeling well rested,
I know it's going to be a
TERRIBLE DAY.

This *is* my happy face.

I could eat well, and exercise,
and get more sleep.

But then I'd feel better.

Being the problem,
not the solution, is a lot

HARDER

than

it

looks.

IT'S WHAT'S FOR DINNER.

You know how it feels like there are always more dirty dishes than clean ones?

Ah, don't you just love that?

LIVE EVERY DAY LIKE IT'S TRASH DAY.

They say you're never fully dressed
without a smile. I say:

UNLESS YOU'RE WEARING
A TRASH CAN!

PART

HOW to
lose FRIENDS
AND
ALIENATE PEOPLE

If you're down in the dumps,

CALL ME.

I'm probably nearby.

You would think it's a lot easier to lose
friends than to make new ones . . .

but let me introduce
you to Elmo.

If you don't have anything nice to say,
COME SIT BY ME.

THAT SOUNDS AWFUL!

Tell me more.

NEVER HUG A GROUCH!

But if you must . . .
don't expect one to hug back.

LOVE THE ONE YOU'RE WITH.

I just hope you're not with me.

A stranger's just a friend

I [DON'T] want to make.

I'm just a grouch,
standing in front of you,
asking you . . .

TO LEAVE ME ALONE!

There's nothing better than
a warm can of trash
and no one to share it with.

LOVE MAY BE BLIND,

but it can smell.

If a smile is a gift,
make sure you give it to me
with a gift receipt.

Looking for a pick-me-up?

YOU can LOOK SOMEWHERE ELSE!

I'm more of a
put-me-down kind of guy.

MORNING PEOPLE ANNOY ME.

So do all other people.

YOUR only **PROBLEM** **IS** your **CAN-DO** attitude.

IT'S NOT YOU, IT'S ME.

But it might also be you.

My favorite friends are the ones who

NEVER CALL

or write or visit.

If you aren't the trash guy, go away.
If you are the trash guy,
just dump everything behind the can.

What's that they say?
Take only memories,

LEAVE ONLY TRASH PILES.

Yeah, pretty sure it was something like that.

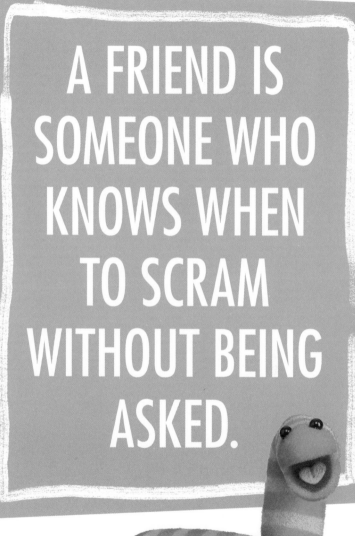

A FRIEND IS SOMEONE WHO KNOWS WHEN TO SCRAM WITHOUT BEING ASKED.

WHAT can I SAY? HE wormed HIS way INTO my LIFE.

PART

WORDS TO

GROUCH BY

If a window of opportunity appears,
some blackout curtains will take care of that.

If your expectations are low enough,
you'll never be disappointed.
That's why I set 'em high. Real high.

One grouch's trash . . .

is another grouch's trash.

EVERY DAY is TRASH DAY WHEN you're A GROUCH.

Nothing's wasted if you
DON'T EVER THROW IT AWAY.

When opportunity knocks,
I pretend

I'M NOT HOME!

Turn that smile upside down.

Follow your bliss—
as long as it takes you

FAR AWAY
FROM
THIS CAN.

When life gives you lemons,
put them in a blender
with rotten tomatoes,
dirty socks,
and old cardboard.

You probably won't even
taste the lemons!

REMEMBER, THE SITUATION COULD ALWAYS BE WORSE.

Just try harder.

Feeling like you're on top of the world?

HEH-HEH.
DON'T LOOK
DOWN.

DON'T CRY OVER SPILLED MILK.

Wait a few days.
Then it will be spoiled milk.
Now, THAT will bring a tear to your eye.

For me, the worst part about feeling down . . .

IS KNOWING IT CAN'T LAST!

GROUCHINESS isn't **EVERYTHING.** **IT'S** the **ONLY** thing.

Since you asked . . .

I **DON'T** know AND I don't care! And **IF** I KNEW, I *STILL* WOULDN'T care!

QUITTERS

NEVER

win.

That works for me.

When one door closes, another one opens.

SLAM THAT ONE SHUT, TOO.

Life is like a box of chocolates.

Too sweet all the time, and it'll make you sick to your stomach.

AIM FOR THE MOON!

Maybe you'll make it.

Whatever, at least you'll
be far away from me.

Can they call you

"GROUCHYPANTS"

when you don't wear pants?

Give the gift that never dies:

STYROFOAM.

Bad moods are temporary.

GROUCHINESS IS FOREVER.

If being grouchy is wrong,

I DON'T WANT TO BE RIGHT!

The best things in life are free.
The better ones are

SMELLY.

Walk a mile in someone else's shoes.
If they have different size feet than yours,

YOU'LL get
REALLY bad
BLISTERS!

YOU MAKE BEING GROUCHY EASY.

I HAVE SOMETHING TO TELL YOU.

Come closer.

Closer.

No, closer . . .

Why does everyone watch sunsets?

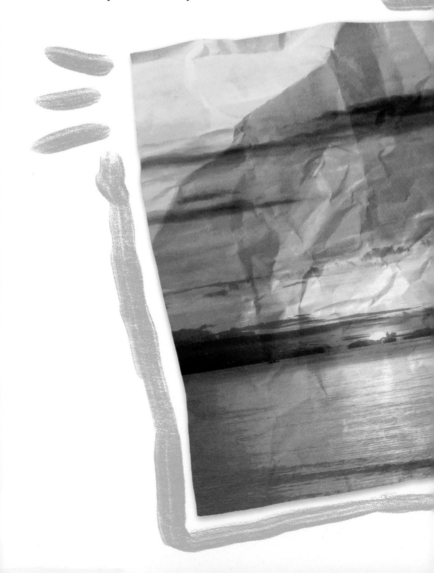

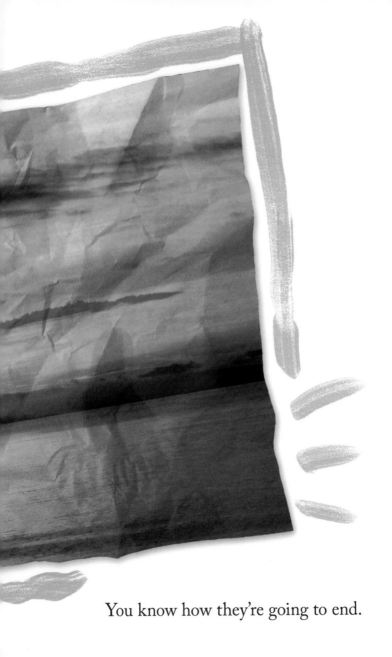

You know how they're going to end.

GROUCHES

gonna

GROUCH.

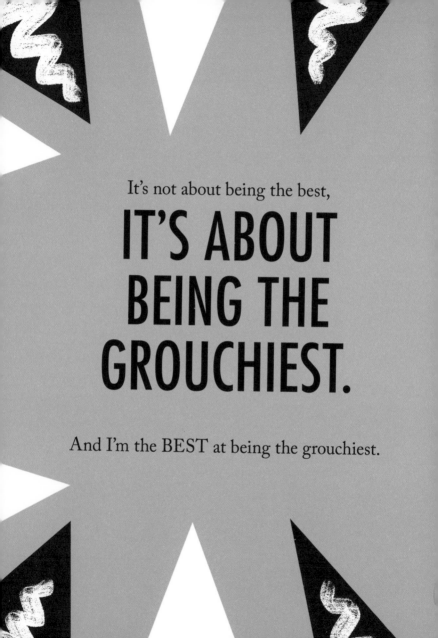

It's not about being the best,

IT'S ABOUT BEING THE GROUCHIEST.

And I'm the BEST at being the grouchiest.

ABOUT THE AUTHOR

Oscar the Grouch doesn't need to explain himself to you.

He lives in a trash can on Sesame Street.

ACKNOWLEDGMENTS

This book wouldn't have been possible
without all of you people making me

SO

GROUCHY

ALL THE TIME.

Don't let the back cover hit you
on the way out.